Dig Yourself Up

Self-published by Leah Stone @leahjstone

Cover art and illustrations | Maggie Moore Setzer
@maggiepaints828

Book design | Rae @inkedneat

ISBN-13: 978-1975948320
ISBN-10: 1975948327

To the people whose footprints
on my heart became the ink on my pages;
and to Z for digging *me* up.

Dig Yourself Up

Contents

from the loving..9

from the loathing..59

from the lusting..105

from the liberation..141

from the loving

Leah Stone

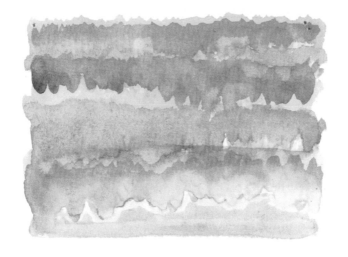

Observe yourself with kind eyes.
Have a little forgiveness.
Mostly for you.

Dig Yourself Up

I lay my hand
on your back
and understand
for the first time
how you can feel
another person's
heartbeat more
than your own.

(Z)

Leah Stone

Walk me through the valley of my past.
Remind me of all the things
I've lost along the way.
Parts of the path are mangled,
but your smile soothes me
all the way home.

Dig Yourself Up

I would trade every lesson
I've ever learned
if you didn't have to be
one of them.

Leah Stone

Love is never without struggle.
But aren't you willing to fight for it,
to bleed for the one thing
that makes you human?
You'll leave with scars and open wounds,
but you'll also leave with someone
to help mend them.

Dig Yourself Up

These bones may keep me upright,
but you keep me standing.

The nape of your
neck was where
my loud mouth
finally found
a worthy silence.

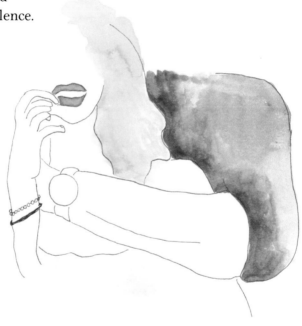

Dig Yourself Up

Eye contact,
invasive and vulnerable
simultaneously.
I wonder when
was the last time
you looked yourself in the eyes
and said something nice?

Leah Stone

You smelled like sunshine.
It filled my nose with hope.
That maybe this something beautiful
would stay.

Dig Yourself Up

I want to feed
the part of you
that you keep trying
to convince yourself
doesn't exist.

Leah Stone

Your words will linger
long after your body leaves.
Water them with love.

Dig Yourself Up

Don't aim to land
a wealthy man.
Try instead for
an honest one.

Leah Stone

I'll let you in
on a little secret:
the people we love
think we are better
than we actually are.
We earn their love
by proving them right
more often than we
prove them wrong.
And just like that,
we actually are better.

Dig Yourself Up

The hardest thing
I ever had to do
was breaking my own heart
just to save it.

Did he complete me?
No.
He did so much more.
He unfolded me.

Dig Yourself Up

The only thing saving me
from this sea of men
is my fellow shipwrecked women
and their bottomless hearts.

And when you stop trying
to measure the moments
in your life based on
other people's opinions,
time will stop
and gift you with
b l i s s.

Dig Yourself Up

Love me
right out of the ocean.
Hair knotted and sandy.
Skin salty and burnt.
Forgive my squinting
as my eyes adjust
to the sight of a man willing
to be my shore.

Leah Stone

She had sunrise intentions
and whiskey dreams,
but I'll be damned
if her smile didn't give me wings.

Dig Yourself Up

I was asked to define motherhood:
as if a piece of your heart
resided outside of your body.

Leah Stone

You know when there's a storm
and just for a moment
the sun peeks between the clouds?
Like it's reminding you
that every feeling is fleeting,
and beauty is only a gust of wind away.

You were my break in the clouds.

Dig Yourself Up

It's true.
I didn't know him that well.
I didn't even know how tall he was,
but I did know
what he sounded like
when he read his favorite book out loud.
Or the way his voice shakes
when he talks about his family.
And if animals can migrate
to find their kind
from thousands of miles away,
through instinct, not a map,
why can't we be the same?

(MJL)

Leah Stone

The best love
is the kind
that mends the wounds
from all the wrong kinds.

Dig Yourself Up

Write me love letters
taped to the bottom
of my coffee mugs.
Speak fondly of my character
even when I don't deserve it.
Love me most when I'm reading.
When I'm being swept up
into a different dimension
and my only worry is how
I'll bring you with me.
I know this is how
I want to be loved because
this is how
I love you.

Leah Stone

If all you ever see in me
is beauty
then I have failed you.
As a friend,
as a lover,
as a human.

Dig Yourself Up

Far away from this place
in the cold quiet of space,
I know the stars pray for us.
That one day we'll stop
putting our pride
before our love.

Leah Stone

'Love hurts'
No.
It is everything
we do to it
that makes it hurt.
Love is pure,
leftover magic from the big bang,
the creation story itself.
The only force powerful enough
to make you the best version of yourself
yet you'd still throw it away
over something that could have
been fixed with an *I'm sorry.*
That's a tragedy.

That's what hurts.

Our love wasn't a fairytale.
It was a short and sweet
bedtime story.
About how love,
in all its majesty
sometimes
is not enough.

Leah Stone

It's kind of you
to offer me your hand,
but I'm much more interested
in your dreams.

Dig Yourself Up

Let me help you
out of that skin.
I'm only concerned
with what it's hiding.

Leah Stone

I knew you were my sky
when your smile became
my sunrise.
I knew I was your star
when at the end of the day
your eyes always landed
on me.

Dig Yourself Up

Time is just an idea.
I've spent years
trapped in-between
sips of coffee,
and I've lost people
like raindrops hitting a roof.
I can't measure life in length,
only in volume;
and I love like the ocean.

Have you ever wondered
what makes lanterns so enchanting?

Because their light shines
from the inside.

Dig Yourself Up

You can't hide from me.
I've lived in your chest cavity.

Leah Stone

I am not a creature
of this forest,
but I can be gentle
if you need me to be.
These murky waters
you pride yourself
on calling home
are hiding just as much
happiness as they are sadness.

There's a shift
from adolescence to adulthood,
a tectonic displacement.
Where you are suddenly
very aware
that everything you love
and everything that loves you
is temporary.

Leah Stone

Every wish,
every prayer,
every curse
I threw at the sky
because no one
ever seems to fit me.
Like a really good pair of leggings
that fit so well you forget
you're wearing them for
three days straight.
Like a drive home,
you don't even have to pay attention.
It's all muscle memory and instinct.
Like reciting every line
of your favorite stupid movie
with your best friend
and a pint, or two, of ice cream.
I want all of it.
Forever.
I am willing to wait.
I am not willing to settle.

Dig Yourself Up

Be my bridge.
Allow me to pass over you
and leave you standing.

Leah Stone

You wrap your arms
around me like shields.
My tears just salty fragments
of redemption.
You whisper into my hair,
"Sometimes you just need
to hear a heartbeat as broken as yours
to know that this hurt
is not the end."

Dig Yourself Up

He walked over me
and left seeds where there
used to be only ash.
He didn't bring the promise
of endless sunshine,
but he did bring
his gardening gloves.
He woke up early every day,
rolled up his sleeves,
and reminded me
that beautiful things
can only grow
when they are well cared for.

Leah Stone

The further I swam
into my own truth,
the more I feared
you were drowning in yours.

Time travel isn't impossible
once you find someone
who makes time stop.

I still find you stirred in my coffee
every morning like sugar.
In my first breath after
swimming in the ocean.
In the tear I've been
holding in for months.
You wait for me
in the moments
I take for granted
but need the most.

Dig Yourself Up

He didn't need
to buy me flowers.
He made us the flowers.

Leah Stone

I have always struggled
with our relationship
as humans between time
and its importance.
Even if our love does last,
our bodies won't.
The ugly truth
of our time here:
the length makes
absolutely no difference.

Dig Yourself Up

I've never been soft.
My skin maybe, but I've
always needed the roughness
of people to make it real.
The rush of you from
my first inhale.
The drop in my serotonin
as soon as you leave the room.
The sting when I realize
you're never coming back.
I live with the volume
all the way up.
It reminds me that all of this
isn't for keeps.

Come.
Sit with me in the soil.
Lay your healing hands
on my thighs and
watch the sun rise.
There could be only this,
only us, if you just come,
quiet your mind, and heal with me.

from the loathing

Leah Stone

I'll sign my goodbye note
in the blood of our dead love.
You don't have to pretend
to be sad about it
because I sure as fuck won't.

Dig Yourself Up

I will stand by my belief
that I deserve someone
who looks at me
the way I used to look at you.
Even ~~if~~
Even though
it isn't you.

Leah Stone

I tried to scream,
but you took my breath
when you shoved my consent
back down my own throat.

Dig Yourself Up

Crack open my chest,
whether by brutal force
or kind gesture;
each time you'll find
it only beats
for the one person
who will never hear it.

You should never have
to break yourself
to make room
for someone else's love.

Dig Yourself Up

Respect him for leaving,
he knew he wasn't enough.
Forgive yourself for loving him anyway,
because loving too hard will never
be a flaw.

Leah Stone

And to think,
I fell for you
under the same sky
that made you
want to leave.

Dig Yourself Up

You were always
trying to read me,
when I've always
been braille.
Craving to be felt
above being seen.

Leah Stone

It might have been enough
that you loved me.
If only you could have seen
past the tip of your dick.

Dig Yourself Up

It takes every drop of courage
to walk away from the things
we love that are also killing us.
Not everything that screams to you
is meant to be heard,
and you can love someone
all the while knowing
they're no good.

Leah Stone

The day is young,
but we're only getting older.
More consumed with our fear
of being alone than caring
for our young.
We make mountains out of molehills
and swipe left on anything
that can't be fixed with
a pill or a blowjob.
And then we wonder why
we need psychedelics to sleep.

Dig Yourself Up

My heart still carries you around
like stones in my pockets.
Only allowing me to stay stagnant
in your putrid memory.
As the days go on,
and they do go on.
With each setting sun
I am a little bit lighter,
a little bit more free.
A little bit less of my blood
screams for you
and it finally reeks of me.

Leah Stone

He fucks your friends
because it's the closest
he can get to the bitch
that was smart enough
to run away,
and he's too lazy
to find a new neighborhood.
I say, let them have it.
Even strays gotta eat.

Dig Yourself Up

You don't get
to stitch me back together this time
just so you can take credit
for the way my eyes shine
when you say my name.
Your love is dosed
in time delayed poison,
and it always hits me
when I think you've changed.

Leah Stone

In a few decades
when you're
still searching
for stale drops of me
at the bottom
of empty bottles,
just remember
my cup is full
without you.

Dig Yourself Up

When you handed me
your dreams and your fears,
I never imagined
you would become both to me.

He digs into me with his lies
not knowing that I am the soil,
needing roots to sustain me.
He wasn't up for my rocky terrain
and I can't settle for someone
who runs from a little quake.

Dig Yourself Up

Like a bee in spring
you went from flower to flower
promising renewal.
When all you wanted
was more practice
at making your sting
feel like love.

Leah Stone

Please.
Don't chisel away at me.
Don't make me choose
between being me
and being yours.
Because I'll pick you,
you'll let me,
and that
is not love.

Dig Yourself Up

I was rabid and starving.
You were dangling
your love like a bone.
But I would rather
be eaten alive
than stay out of need
and not desire.

Leah Stone

And I think
I would drink
a case of you
if only
the taste of you
wouldn't make me
hate myself
in the morning.

Dig Yourself Up

Your whiskey induced confessions
would mean so much more
if you cared enough
to remember them
in the morning.

Leah Stone

I wanted you.
I waited for you.
I got you.
I wished with you.

And none of it
prepared me
to lose you.

Dig Yourself Up

Is anything about you real?
Or have you forgotten
what life looks like
sans airbrush?

Leah Stone

So I slipped out
of our love
like a dress
that was so beautiful,
but had always been
too tight.

Dig Yourself Up

He smiled at me
and handed me back
all my broken pieces.
The only thing
he ever gave me
that was worth a damn.

Leah Stone

Let's get one thing straight:
I allow you to sit
in the sunshine of my love.
I can burn you as quickly
as I grew you,
boy.

Dig Yourself Up

I could drive to your house
in my sleep.
Shit, I could probably walk,
but I've learned to stay away
from people who only see me
when I am at their feet.

Leah Stone

I couldn't feel the weight
of your words
because there wasn't anything
left in your eyes that
I recognized.

Dig Yourself Up

We kept running into each other...

never on the same page.

Leah Stone

Your hands used to hold me
like the sky held the stars.
Now they are as cold
as a headstone
and they read:
what could have been.

Dig Yourself Up

I could hold on forever
but I won't.
It still wouldn't
be long enough,
and you still wouldn't
deserve me.

Leah Stone

It is always in silence
that your memory screams.

Dig Yourself Up

You could devour me
line by line,
and you still wouldn't see
my pen bleeds for you.

Leah Stone

I could tell you that I secretly love the pain.
How I like my showers so hot
that I cringe when I get in.
Something about the burn
makes me feel clean.
Or how I look for home
in handfuls of other people's hair.
And no matter who rolls over
and says *good morning*
it's never you, not anymore.
I could tell you that I love it,
but honestly it feels so fucking good
compared to nothing at all.

Dig Yourself Up

Beware:
the man with countless stories
and not one worthy memory.

Leah Stone

You had me in your palm
and I was too small,
not challenging enough.
So I stood up
and you couldn't manage
the competition.
So let's clear it up:
I will always need me
more than I need you.

Dig Yourself Up

You sold your soul
to make more sense
to the world,
and now you're not worth
your weight in memories.

Leah Stone

I am not
an abandoned house
here for you to meander
in and out of as you please.
I am the foundation.
Ready to be built upon
with honest hands.

Dig Yourself Up

It was over the moment
I wasn't afraid to lose you.
I was more scared of what
would happen to me
if I didn't.

Your roots are too plentiful
to take hold in a greedy heart.

We loved.
So hard.
Then crashed.
And burned.
Broken promises.
Cave in.
You call.
I crumble.
Rinse Repeat.

from the lusting

Leah Stone

I can only handle
a moanful of your love
at once, anything more
feels greedy.

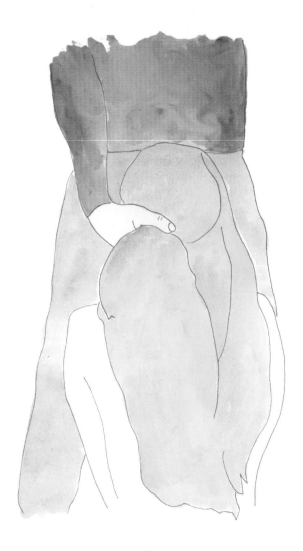

Dig Yourself Up

Don't hide your venom from me.
I like the burn.

Leah Stone

I'm the kind of woman
who sneaks out
in the middle of the night.
You look so peaceful
bathed in moonlight.

But as soon as the sun
hits your face
you appear far too hopeful
and all I want to do is

                                                            run.

Dig Yourself Up

I don't bump
into people.
I crash.
Hard.
I knock
the both of us out,
and wake up
covered in bruises.
Asking myself why
and asking you
for more.

Leah Stone

He laid me down
only to cover me up
and admire my mind.
He traced the curve
of my nose with his fingers
and breathed me in like
I was the last rose on earth.
He asked why I write
so often about love
when in truth
we've never met face to face.
I replied honestly,
what else is there?

Dig Yourself Up

I found a man
buried in the sand
of my expectations.
My favorite parts of him
tasted of salt and they burn
in the only way that doesn't kill,
it ignites.
His hair smelled like pine
and I swear the sap he spoke
turned my whole body into a river.

Leah Stone

In a world
where only
sight matters,
be pitch black.
So people can only
feel you.

Dig Yourself Up

How do you expect
anyone to see you
beyond face value
if your surface
is what you value most
about yourself?

Leah Stone

I lay with my back on the shore.
Hips digging into your coarse chin.
Legs crashing around your shoulders.
And the waves
Just.
Kept.
Coming.

Dig Yourself Up

I let him tear into me
night after night,
like a lion digging
into his meal.
Trying to fuck
all those holes
in his heart full.
The sad truth:
my body would recover.
He would not.

Leah Stone

You slide two fingers into my mouth,
tasting vaguely like my center of gravity.
Every particle in the universe
standing still to watch our collide.

Suddenly my only concern
is how to consume all of you
at once, while we make
the cosmos watch.

Dig Yourself Up

I'll be your fix.
Take a nice
long
hard
hit.
Careful though.
The come
down is a
bitch.

Leah Stone

Your lips were so full
like the moon,
as they set sail
on my horizon.
You and I
always did best
on the dark side.

Dig Yourself Up

Your love drips onto me like paint.
Daring my charcoal heart
to be smothered by the color
that lingered in your brush.

Leah Stone

Get lost in me
as I drift into your eyes.
Can we just swim
in this ignorance
knowing it's a lie?

Dig Yourself Up

Something about the way
he drank his whiskey.
Each sip like a breath.
It made me wonder
what he could do
with a bed
and a mouthful of me.

Leah Stone

Wreck me.
I've been far
too comfortable
in this life
waiting for someone
like you.

Dig Yourself Up

I wish I could tell you
I was the type to go willingly,
but I always put up a fight.
Even when it feels good.
The bite just comes naturally.

Leah Stone

You want me to tell you
that it's okay to hate him.
For leaving,
for staying,
for being too good of a fuck.
But you fell for it, or didn't.
Pick yourself up from the bathtub
that is your past, and dry off.
Don't worry.
I'm sure someone will be by
to break your heart tomorrow.

Dig Yourself Up

Just because most women
fall at your feet for only
a moan of your time,
don't expect me to go so easily.
I do rails of pixie dust
and bathe in bad intentions.
Your lucky charms are no match
for my magic.

Leah Stone

They pin my hands
behind my back
hoping my rise in adrenaline
will make me ignore
that their hand trembles.
You can back me into a cage
but I am not the bull,
and I must say
that scruff on your chin
looks like a mighty fine place
to sit.

Dig Yourself Up

I saw strategy in your eyes
as if loving me was a game.
When I just needed you to see
that I'm the prize.

Leah Stone

Don't fight the crashing waves.
It's a losing battle.
Love does not need persuasion.
It is sure.

Dig Yourself Up

His hands were forces of nature.
They dove into me and I was lost.
Not like being lost in the open ocean,
but like being trapped underwater
and still being able to breathe.

Leah Stone

Wrap your promises
around me like flames.
I usually don't mind a chill,
but tonight.
Tonight.
I'm
just
so
cold.

Dig Yourself Up

Lying:
The second best thing
you did with your mouth.

Leah Stone

My face might look prettier
with a smile painted on it,
and yours might look better in my lap.
Let's not assume, okay?

Dig Yourself Up

You scorch through my veins
like only something
that's bad for me can.

Leah Stone

You were my favorite ghost story.
A man born into madness
and scraped across the coals of humanity.
If demons could talk, yours would roar.
But what a beautiful song we made
when you dull it down to a pur.

Dig Yourself Up

It's crazy how often sex
has nothing to do with fucking someone,
and how loving the wrong person
can leave you with no love for yourself.

I can level you
with this mouth of mine.
Whether with these iron words
forged under the pressure of
an aged heart or with the lips
I've known how to use for too long.
I will have you on your knees regardless.

Dig Yourself Up

Coming for you
was like arriving home
to a place I had never been,
but had been yearning for
my whole life.

Leah Stone

You always kiss me
when my mouth is full of questions.
You didn't want to say it,
but we both knew
you weren't going to stay.

from the liberation

Dig Yourself Up

Leah Stone

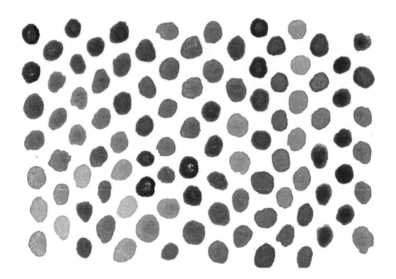

Expel me of my humanity.
Let me be light
and ready to bound into life
without my worry to overcome me.
Liberate me of sadness.
Leave me at nirvana.
So that I may frolic
and bask in its freedom.

Dig Yourself Up

Embrace these truths:
You know nothing for certain,
this is the fun in it.
Dreams grow better in positive soil.
Any tree that now shades us
had to survive hundreds of storms
just to get here.

Leah Stone

You have a choice
every day
to fill your cup
of happiness
or spill it.
Which sounds better to you?

Dig Yourself Up

Some people talk of yesterdays
because it's all they have to define them.
They speak poorly of others
because they don't like themselves.
Let them stew in their hate.
You are much too full of hope
for that nonsense.

Leah Stone

If you have to bury other women
under the dirt
to make yourself seem
more beautiful:
you're a weed,
not a flower.

Why fake it?
Smiles,
friendship,
orgasms.
Your people are out there
waiting to love you,
just the way you come.
Stop making excuses.
Go fucking find them.

Leah Stone

And you.
You scare the shit
out of people.
With your iron heart,
blood under your nails,
and stars in your eyes.
But I swear that fire
in your heart is not the lie.
Their fear is.

That weight atop
your shoulders
was only meant
to teach you,
not cripple you.

Leah Stone

I keep you at arm's length
because my walls can only crumble
from within.
Entrance is earned.

Dig Yourself Up

You can't be stone
all the time.
There is monumental
strength
in crumbling;
it shows what
you're made of.

Leah Stone

Be stardust
in a world of
imitation glitter.

Dig Yourself Up

Give yourself a moment
to grieve the person that you've lost.
The friend, the partner, the lover.
Give yourself the time you need
to let them die,
and become a memory
instead of a trigger.

Leah Stone

Breathe me in or breathe me out.
I've been left in the dark before,
the wilderness doesn't scare me.

Why
would
you
settle
yourself
for
someone
who
doesn't
move

you?

Leah Stone

Let things fall just shy
of being *together.*
I promise it's more fun
that way.

You can only be
as beautiful
as the people
who water you.

Leah Stone

There is no badge of honor
in holding onto someone
who wouldn't notice
if you were gone.
Let. Go.

People are constantly
showing you who they are.
Growth is set in motion
by our acknowledgment
of these actions.

Leah Stone

Always accept the challenge of proving
that you can bloom
despite other people's bullshit.

Dig Yourself Up

Stop looking for the shiny people.
They don't actually exist.
You want the thrift store memories,
the smoke break confessions.
The people who know
every word to every song,
and they laugh like
it makes them fucking rich.
These are the people
that will teach you.

Leah Stone

Don't worry about
outgrowing your pot,
as long as you're growing
towards the sun.

Dig Yourself Up

Little girl
you can bring this world
to its knees, if only you
smile politely and say
FUCK YOU
to every single thing it tells
you to be.

Leah Stone

I hope you question everything.
Don't accept an answer that doesn't
sit well in your gut.
Dig a little deeper.
Scratch a little harder.
Read the weird books
with the ugly covers.
Talk to people who don't agree
with everything you say.
And please,
never stop surprising yourself.

Dig Yourself Up

See the lesson
where others
can only see
the break.

Leah Stone

Stop feeling obligated
to do things that make you unhappy.
Don't go to that party.
You've never liked that girl.
Don't act like he never mattered.
He did, but he's gone now.
It's your turn to fall in love again.
This time, with yourself.

Dig Yourself Up

It ended a long time ago.
But it was over
the moment you said
please
I said
no
and it didn't hurt at all.
It was like breathing,
and I could only do it
without you.

Leah Stone

You can find me
on the precipice
of love lost
and found glory.
I've lived too long
in the shadows
to ever stray
from the sunshine again.

Dig Yourself Up

Dance in the ruins
of your heartache.
You'll find pieces
of yourself in the soil
you've waited far too long
to meet.

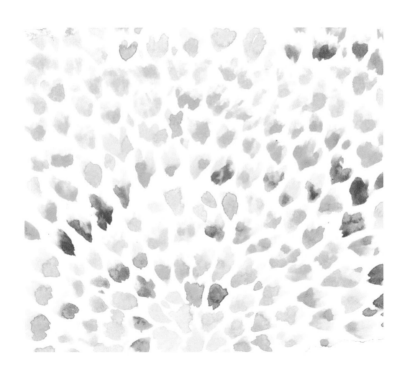

Leah Stone

I find little pieces of you
sprinkled in all the things
I used to love.
90's sitcoms,
box wine,
back rubs,
sleeping in on Sunday mornings.
Of all those things,
I used to miss you the most.
Now the thought of finding
new things to love
brought me excitement
instead of fear.

Patience is a virtue
best reserved
for self care.
Repeat daily.

Leah Stone

Love me, hate me, fuck me?
Just do it better
than I do myself.
Anything less
is settling.

Dig Yourself Up

To be a woman
is to be *too* something
at the expense of something else.
So here is the only truth that matters:
You are too important
to be bound by the limitations of
someone else's expectations.

Leah Stone

Happiness is an
endless candle
inside of you,
dim but steady.
Sadness is a forest fire,
engulfing and beautiful
in its own right.
It is easier to succumb
to the forest
than it is to maintain the flame.
Be happy anyway.

Learn from the currents.
The act of moving on
while remaining whole.

Leah Stone

There is a woman
inside of me
who is quiet.
She is satisfied at her
own reflection
and her curiosity
does not get
the best of her.
She had to die.
So my words could
live.

Dig Yourself Up

Your heart doesn't fit
in their hand
because that is never
where it was supposed to land.

Your mistake is assuming
that the truth alone
will bring you peace.
The truth is the same
as any other excuse.
It will not ease the ache.
It will only give it a name.

Dig Yourself Up

We wrap people's love around us
like it's the only thing that can make us whole;
but unless it starts with yourself
it might as well be a noose.

Leah Stone

Honor the place between
heartache and healed.
This gray area will breathe
color back into your bones.

Dig Yourself Up

I am a nightmare
of a woman
whose only daydream
is of a fairytale.

Leah Stone

Why is it important
for women
to tell women
that they're beautiful:
because in this life,
that only seems
to be deemed true
if a man's hands
are groping it.
I say we take that word back,
and use it *on* each other
instead of *against* each other.

Dig Yourself Up

I am ~~still~~
I am always
learning to hold
the parts of me
that no one else does.

Leah Stone

I flip through old journals
and wave to the versions
of myself I've thrown
to the wind.
I tell myself,
you've survived
all of this before.
Stand up woman.
Try again.

Dig Yourself Up

As a child,
you must go from crawling
on your hands and knees
begging for guidance
to standing on your
own two feet.
The same is true
for becoming a woman.

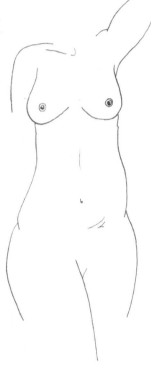

Leah Stone

You loved my cover
and tightly bound spine.
But you were always too afraid
to read me, in fear
you were only a chapter.
And for so many other reasons:

You weren't even a footnote.

Dig Yourself Up

You want anger?
I've got some tucked
in my t-shirt drawer
in the form of a letter
I never sent to the man
who raped me.
You want regret?
Follow me through the cemetery
to talk to my friends
buried in the ground.
You want passion?
Just watch me in a coffee shop
fucking the shit out a piece of paper
with my pen.
You want nostalgia?
How about every time I look at my daughter
and see the love I used to share
with her father?
These are the things that
have happened to me.
This is NOT who I am.

Leah Stone

Bury them.
The same thing
they did to you.
Forgive them.
Because they
are only human, too.

Dig Yourself Up

Those first few years of your twenties
fly by like the clouds on a day
you forget to look up.
As you roar into your mid twenties
you start to feel the first signs of age.
A cracking knee as you rise in the mornings.
A muscle in your neck spasms
when you reach for your seat belt.
Those smiles start to chart your face
like the shoreline after a storm.
Worn.
You wake up already tired.
Silence becomes pornographic,
and validation starts with your
good morning to the mirror.
These are all signs of life.
Foot prints on your path here,
solely your own.
Some of them ache.
Some of them shine.
They are all beautiful.
And I've buried too many
twenty-somethings
to think of this clock
as a curse.

Leah Stone

If this monthly flood
between my legs
makes you uncomfortable,
maybe I should remind you
where the fuck you come from.
Because as much as I know
our pain causes you discomfort,
you sure as hell don't seem
to like it when people
poke fun at your organs.

Dig Yourself Up

It is in these moments
I feel most at peace.
Surrounded by my friends,
our old road trip cd's,
and our cheap wine.
Sitting in a circle,
laughing about nothing,
wanting absolutely **nothing**
but one another's company.

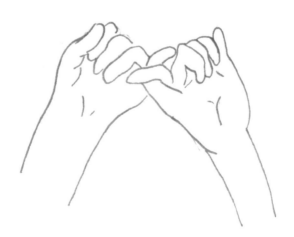

Leah Stone

And now you hate me
because without you
I am worth so much more.

Dig Yourself Up

I smelled sin on his skin
and he told me he loved
watching the stars burn themselves
to bits every night.
I smiled and replied,
you are asking an Aries woman
to run from a fire
when she was born from it.

Leah Stone

I walk outside
and try to experience it
like new every day.
Life lessons await me in the breeze,
raindrops cascading down my window
share my sorrow.
And the sunshine,
the glorious sunshine
radiates my love.

I am not a hurricane.
I am the tree built
to withstand it.
I am not a wildflower.
I am the grass.
Growing despite abuse.
I am not a mermaid.
I am the sea.
A home to those
who believe in magic.

Leah Stone

Most men just watch our lips move
up and down with their imagination.
Condemning women as the sacrifice
to humankind's obsession with lust.
As if our bodies are anything
besides just that.
We didn't earn them,
we didn't ask for them.
But we have the right to be
in charge of them.
Yet every action
set in motion
by the softness of our skin
and the warmth of our insides
is blamed on us.
You want us to be both
angel and siren.
We were asking for it, right?
Well we were also
born with brains
and I'm calling
BULLSHIT.

Dig Yourself Up

Big
brave
heart,
it is okay
to be scared
too.

Leah Stone

Nothing will make people
hate you more
than not being
exactly like them.
Stay weird.

Dig Yourself Up

I stopped judging my body
the moment I realized
it doesn't judge me
for my misuse of it.

Leah Stone

Pain is inevitable.
Find someone
who makes
that fact bearable.
Better yet,
let that someone
be you.

Dig Yourself Up

She didn't walk on water.
She much preferred
the rawness of people
rather than the reality.
It almost always
hurt her in the end
but it made the moments
that weighed the most
easier to carry.

Leah Stone

Oh.
Did my cockiness
upset you?
I didn't notice.
I try not to concern myself
with the opinions
of men whose dicks
are smaller than mine.

Dig Yourself Up

Sometimes she learned from the moon.
Only to expose herself so fully in moderation,
because the world went mad
when she reached her apex.

Leah Stone

Have you ever noticed that men
never apologize for being confident?
So why should we?
If you're going to be
passionate about anything:
let it be yourself.

Dig Yourself Up

I'm really tired of everyone pretending
that sadness doesn't cleanse you
just as much as happiness does.

Leah Stone

Wash me ashore already.
I've been drowning
in other people's expectations.

Dig Yourself Up

I used to second guess myself constantly.
I would look into my own eyes
and question the color.
Everyone always tells me
they're brown but
right after I cry they scream green.
Blades of grass wrapping around my pupil
like they're smelling lavender for the first time.
I breathe in the flowers
that have always clung to my ears
and hear the sound of my childhood: laughter.
No one tells me what I am.

We're all smiles and mangled roots.
Dig yourself up. I dare you.

Acknowledgements

To Kenzie, for being my little sunspot.
To Hailey, my martian.
To Mom, for reminding me that the light is
always there whether you can see it or not.
To Dad, for always letting me be me.
To Marge, my first friend, for making
weird the new black.
To Raven, for showing me that
words are home.
To Michael, for making me believe again.

Lastly, to the writers I've met along the way.
Who inspire me, captivate me, and remind
me why we do this. You know who you are.
Don't ever stop bleeding that ink.

About the Author

Leah Stone was born and raised in Raleigh, North Carolina. In the short period of time that she has been using Instagram as her writing platform, she has undoubtedly become one of the most well-known names on social media. She began her journey at a young age writing for herself and realized instantly that she had found her calling. As a writer, Leah is most known for being able to express her perspective on issues that all women are facing, in a raw, relatable, and empowering fashion. In her free time, you'll probably find her at home dancing around the kitchen with her daughter, or somewhere around town writing and drinking iced coffee. Between her witty personality and strong stance on female equality, she has easily and unknowingly become everyone's favorite feminist.

Made in the USA
Lexington, KY
16 June 2018